A CHILD IS BORN

A Modern Drama of the Nativity

By
STEPHEN VINCENT BENET

Stephen Vincent Benét

Stephen Vincent Benét was born on 22nd July 1898 in Bethlehem, Pennsylvania, United States.

Benét was sent to the Hitchcock Military Academy at the age of ten and then continued his education at The Albany Academy in New York. He also attended Yale University where he received his M.A. in English.

Benét was an accomplished writer at an early age, having had his first book published at 17 and submitting his third volume of poetry in lieu of a thesis for his degree. During his time at Yale, he was an influential figure at the 'Yale Lit' literary magazine, and a fellow member of the Elizabethan Club. Benét was also a part-time contributor for the early Time Magazine.

Benét's involvement with the University literary scene led to a decade-long judgeship of the Yale Series of Younger Poets Competition. He is also responsible for publishing the first volumes of work by authors such as James Agee, Muriel Rukeyser, Jeremy Ingalls, and Margaret Walker. In 1931, he was elected as a fellow of the American Academy of Arts ad Sciences.

Benét's best known works are the book-length narrative poem *American Civil War, John Brown's Body* (1928), for which he won a Pulitzer Prize in 1929, and two short stories, *The Devil and Daniel Webster* (1936) and *By the Waters of Babylon* (1937). Benét won a second Pulitzer Prize posthumously for his unfinished poem *Western Star* in 1944.

Stephen Vincent Benét died of a heart attack in New York City, on 13th March, 1943, and is buried in Evergreen Cemetery, Stonington, Conneticut.

Prayer

God of the free, we pledge our hearts and lives today to the cause of all free mankind.

Grant us victory over the tyrants who would enslave all free men and nations. Grant us faith and understanding to cherish all those who fight for freedom as if they were our brothers. Grant us brotherhood in hope and union, not only for the space of this bitter war, but for the days to come which shall and must unite all the children of earth.

Our earth is but a small star in the great universe. Yet of it we can make, if we choose, a planet unvexed by war, untroubled by hunger or fear, undivided by senseless distinction of race, color or theory. Grant us that courage and foreseeing to begin this task today that our children and our children's children may be proud of the name of man.

The spirit of man has awakened and the soul of man has gone forth. Grant us the wisdom and the vision to comprehend the greatness of man's spirit, that suffers and endures so hugely for a goal beyond his own brief span. Grant us honor for our dead who died in the faith, honor for our living who work and strive for the faith, redemption and security for all captive lands and peoples. Grant us patience with the deluded and pity for the betrayed. And grant us the skill and valor that shall cleanse the world of oppression and the old base doctrine that the strong must eat the weak because they are strong.

Yet most of all grant us brotherhood, not only for this day but for all our years—a brotherhood not of words but of acts and deeds. We are all of us children of earth—

grant us that simple knowledge. If our brothers are oppressed, then we are oppressed. If they hunger, we hunger. If their freedom is taken away, our freedom is not secure. Grant us a common faith that man shall know bread and peace—that he shall know justice and righteousness, freedom and security, an equal opportunity and an equal chance to do his best, not only in our own lands, but throughout the world. And in that faith let us march toward the clean world our hands can make. Amen.

NOTE

Mr. Archibald MacLeish, poet and Librarian of Congress, asked Mr. Benét to write THE UNITED NATIONS PRAYER to be used in connection with the celebration of Flag Day, 1942. It was incorporated in President Franklin D. Roosevelt's Flag Day speech over an international network on the evening of June 14th.

A CHILD IS BORN is a modern drama of the Nativity written for the program, "Cavalcade of America," and broadcast over the National Broadcasting Company's network on the night of December 21, 1942. In the original cast Alfred Lunt played the part of the Innkeeper and Lynn Fontanne played the Innkeeper's Wife. Other featured players were:

NARRATOR	Carl Frank
LEAH	Charita Bauer
SARAH	Ann Thomas
JOSEPH OF NAZARETH	Kenneth Delmar
DISMAS, A THIEF	Frank Readick
PREFECT	Everett Sloane

The play was so successful that it was repeated by popular request on the same program on the evening of December 20, 1943 with Helen Hayes and Philip Merivale in the leading roles.

A Child Is Born

CAST OF CHARACTERS

NARRATOR
THE INNKEEPER
THE INNKEEPER'S WIFE
LEAH
SARAH } Servants at the inn
A SOLDIER
JOSEPH OF NAZARETH
DISMAS, A THIEF
VOICE OF A PREFECT
VOICES OF SOLDIERS AND OFFICERS
VOICES OF KINGS
VOICES OF SHEPHERDS

SCENE: The kitchen of an inn. There is a flight of stairs leading to the rooms above. The door of the kitchen opens on the street.

[*Music, as broadcast opens. It fades. Narrator speaks.*]

NARRATOR. I'm your narrator. It's my task to say
Just where and how things happen in our play,
Set the bare stage with words instead of props
And keep on talking till the curtain drops.
So you shall know, as well as our poor skill
Can show you, whether it is warm or chill,
Indoors or out, a battle or a fair,
In this, our viewless theater of the air.
It's an old task—old as the human heart,
Old as those bygone players and their art
Who, in old days when faith was nearer earth,
Played out the mystery of Jesus' birth
In hall or village green or market square
For all who chose to come and see them there,
And, if they knew that Herod, in his crown,
Was really Wat, the cobbler of the town,
And Tom, the fool, played Abraham the Wise,
They did not care. They saw with other eyes.
The story was their own—not far away,
As real as if it happened yesterday,
Full of all awe and wonder yet so near,
A marvelous thing that could have happened here
In their own town—a star that could have blazed
On their own shepherds, leaving them amazed,
Frightened and questioning and following still
To the bare stable—and the miracle.

So we, tonight, who are your players too,
Ask but to tell that selfsame tale to you
In our own words, the plain and simple speech
Of human beings, talking each to each,
Troubled with their own cares, not always wise,
And yet, at moments, looking toward the skies.

The time is—time. The place is anywhere.
The voices speak to you across the air
To say that once again a child is born.
A child is born.
"I pray you all, give us your audience
And hear this matter with reverence."
   [*Music*]
There is a town where men and women live
Their lives as people do in troubled times,
Times when the world is shaken. There is an inn.
A woman sings there in the early morning.
   [*Music, fading into the voice of a woman—the inn-
   keeper's wife—singing as she goes about her house-
   hold tasks*]

   INNKEEPER'S WIFE. In Bethlehem of Judea
There shall be born a child,
A child born of woman
And yet undefiled.

He shall not come to riches,
To riches and might,
But in the bare stable
He shall be Man's light.

He shall not come to conquest,
The conquest of kings,
But in the bare stable
He shall judge all things.

King Herod, King Herod,
Now what will you say
Of the child in the stable
This cold winter day?

I hear the wind blowing
Across the bare thorn,
I fear not King Herod
If this child may be born.

> [*Sound of steps coming down a flight of stone stairs. A man's voice, rough and suspicious—the voice of the innkeeper. The innkeeper is middle-aged—his wife somewhat younger*]

INNKEEPER. Singing again! I told you not to sing!

WIFE. I'm sorry. I forgot.

INNKEEPER. Forgot? That's fine!
That's wonderful! That answers everything!
The times are hard enough and bad enough
For anyone who tries to keep an inn,
Get enough bread to stick in his own mouth
And keep things going, somehow, in his town.
The country's occupied. We have no country.
You've heard of that, perhaps?
You've seen their soldiers, haven't you? You know
Just what can happen to our sort of people
Once there's a little trouble? Answer me!

WIFE [*wearily*]. I've seen. I know.

INNKEEPER. You've seen. You know. And you keep singing songs!
Not ordinary songs—the kind of songs
That might bring in a little bit of trade,
Songs with a kind of pleasant wink in them
That make full men forget the price of the wine,
The kind of songs a handsome girl can sing
After their dinner to good customers
—And, thanks to me, the inn still has a few!—

Oh no! You have to sing rebellious songs
About King Herod!

    WIFE. I'm sorry. I forgot.

    INNKEEPER. Sorry? Forgot? You're always saying
that!
Is it your business what King Herod does?
Is it your place to sing against King Herod?

    WIFE. I think that he must be a wicked man,
A very wicked man.

    INNKEEPER. Oh, la, la, la!
Sometimes *I* think your ways will drive me mad.
Are you a statesman or a general?
Do you pretend to know the ins and outs
Of politics and why the great folk do
The things they do—and why we have to bear them?
Because it's we—we—we
Who have to bear them, first and last and always,
In every country and in every time.
They grind us like dry wheat between the stones.
Don't you know that?

    WIFE. I know that, somehow, kings
Should not be wicked and grind down the people.
I know that kings like Herod should not be.

    INNKEEPER. All right—all right. I'm not denying
that.
I'm reasonable enough. I know the world.
I'm willing to admit to anyone
At least behind closed doors
    [*He drops his voice*]
That Herod isn't quite my sort of king
And that I don't approve of all he does.

Still, there he is. He's king. How will it help
If I go out and write on someone's wall
    [*In a whisper*]
"Down with King Herod!"
    [*His voice comes up again*]
What's it worth?
The cross for me, the whipping post for you,
The inn burned down, the village fined for treason,
Just because one man didn't like King Herod.
For that's the way things are.

    WIFE. Yet there are men—

    INNKEEPER. Oh yes, I know—fanatics, rabble, **fools**,
Outcasts of war, misfits, rebellious souls,
Seekers of some vague kingdom in the stars—
They hide out in the hills and stir up trouble,
Call themselves prophets, too, and prophesy
That something new is coming to the world,
The Lord knows what!
    Well, it's a long time coming,
And, meanwhile, we're the wheat between the stones.

    WIFE. Something must come.

    INNKEEPER. Believe it if you choose,
But, meantime, if we're clever, we can live
And even thrive a little—clever wheat
That slips between the grinding stones and grows
In little green blade-sprinkles on the ground.
At least, if you'll not sing subversive songs
To other people but your poor old husband.
    [*Changing tone*]
Come, wife, I've got some news.
I didn't mean to be so angry with you.
You've some queer fancies in that head of yours

—Lord, don't I know!—but you're still the tall girl
With the grave eyes and the brook-running voice
I took without a dower or a price
Out of your father's house because—oh, well—
Because you came. And they've not been so bad,
The years since then. Now have they?

    WIFE. No.

    INNKEEPER. That's right.
Give us a kiss.
    [*Pause*]
        I couldn't help the child.
I know you think of that, this time of year.
He was my son, too, and I think of him.
I couldn't help his dying.

    WIFE. No, my husband.

    INNKEEPER. He stretched his little arms to me and
        died.
And yet I had the priest—the high priest, too.
I didn't spare the money.

    WIFE. No, my husband.
I am a barren bough. I think and sing
And am a barren bough.

    INNKEEPER. Oh, come, come, come!

    WIFE. The fault is mine. I had my joyous season,
My season of full ripening and fruit
And then the silence and the aching breast.
I thought I would have children. I was wrong,
But my flesh aches to think I do not have them.
I did not mean to speak of this at all.
I do not speak of it. I will be good.
There is much left—so much.

The kindness and the bond that lasts the years
And all the small and treasurable things
That make up life and living. Do not care
So much. I have forgotten. I'll sing softly,
Not sing at all. It was long past and gone.
Tell me your news. Is it good news?

    INNKEEPER [*eagerly*]. The best!
The prefect comes to dinner here tonight
With all his officers—oh yes, I know,
The enemy—of course, the enemy—
But someone has to feed them.

    WIFE. And they'll pay?

    INNKEEPER. Cash.

    WIFE. On the nail?

    INNKEEPER. Yes.

    WIFE. Good.

    INNKEEPER. I thought you'd say so.
Oh, we'll make no great profit—not tonight—
I've seen the bill of fare they asked of me,
Quails, in midwinter! Well, we'll give them—quails!
And charge them for them, too! You know the trick?

    WIFE. Yes.

    INNKEEPER. They must be well served. I'll care for that,
The honest innkeeper, the thoughtful man,
Asking, "Your worship, pray another glass
Of our poor wine! Your worship, is the roast
Done to your worship's taste? Oh, nay, nay, nay,
Your worship, all was settled in the bill,

So do not spoil my servants with largesse,
Your worship!"—And he won't. He pinches pennies.
But, once he's come here, he will come again,
And we shall live, not die, and put some coin,
Some solid, enemy and lovely coin
Under the hearthstone, eh?
Spoil the Egyptians, eh?
    [*He laughs*]
That's my war and my battle and my faith.
The war of every sane and solid man
And, even if we have no child to follow us,
It shall be won, I tell you!
    [*There is a knock at the outer door*]
Hark! What's that?
I'll go—the maids aren't up yet—lazybones!
    [*The knock is repeated, imperatively*]

    INNKEEPER [*grumbling*]. A minute—just a minute!
It's early yet—you needn't beat the door down.
This is an honest inn.
    [*He shoots the bolts and opens the door, while speaking*]
Good morning.

    SOLDIER'S VOICE. Hail Cæsar! Are you keeper of this inn?

    INNKEEPER. Yes, sir.

    SOLDIER. Orders from the prefect. No other guests shall be entertained at your inn tonight after sundown. The prefect wishes all the rooms to be at the disposal of his guests.

    INNKEEPER. All the rooms?

    SOLDIER. You understand plain Latin, don't you?

INNKEEPER. Yes, sir, but—

SOLDIER. Well?

INNKEEPER. Sir, when the prefect first commanded
me,
There was a party of my countrymen
Engaged for a small room—he'd hear no noise—
No noise at all—

SOLDIER. This is the prefect's feast—the Saturnalia—
You've heard your orders.

INNKEEPER. Yes, sir. Yes, indeed, sir.

SOLDIER. See they are carried out! No other guests!
Hail Cæsar!

INNKEEPER [*feebly*]. Hail Cæsar!
[*He slams the door*]
Well, that's pleasant.
All rooms at the disposal of the prefect!
No other guests! I'll have to warn Ben-Ezra.
But he's a sound man—he will understand.
We'll cook his mutton here and send it to him
And the wine, too—a bottle of good wine—
The second best and let the prefect pay for it!
That will make up. No other guests. Remember
No other guests!

WIFE. I will remember.

INNKEEPER. Do so.
It is an order. Now, about the quail.
You'll make the sauce. That's the important thing.
A crow can taste like quail, with a good sauce.
You have your herbs?

WIFE. Yes.

INNKEEPER. Well then, begin, begin!
It's morning and we haven't too much time
And the day's bitter cold. Well, all the better.
They'll drink the more but—all this work to do
And the fire barely started! Sarah! Leah!
Where are those lazy servants? Where's the fish?
Where's the new bread? Why haven't we begun?
Leah and Sarah, come and help your mistress!
I'll rouse the fools! There's work to do today!
>   [*He stamps up the stairs. She moves about her business.*]

>   WIFE [*singing*]. In Bethlehem of Judea
There was an inn also.
There was no room within it
For any but the foe.

No child might be born there.
No bud come to bloom.
For there was no chamber
And there was no room.
>   [*Her voice fades off into music which swells up and down*]

>   NARRATOR. And the day passed and night fell on the town,
Silent and still and cold. The houses lay
Huddled and dark beneath the watching stars
And only the inn windows streamed with light—
>   [*Fade into offstage noise of a big party going on upstairs*]

>   1ST VOICE [*offstage*]. Ha, ha, ha! And then the Cilician said to the Ethiopian. He said—

2ND VOICE [*offstage*]. Well, I remember when we first took over Macedonia. There was a girl there—

3RD VOICE [*offstage*]. Quiet, gentlemen, quiet—the prefect wishes to say a few words—

PREFECT'S VOICE [*off*]. Gentlemen—men of Rome—mindful of Rome's historic destiny—and of our good friend King Herod—who has chosen alliance with Rome rather than a useless struggle—keep them under with a firm hand—

SARAH. What is he saying up there?

LEAH. I don't know.
I don't know the big words. The soldier said—

SARAH. You and your soldier!

LEAH. Oh, he's not so bad.
He brought me a trinket—see!

SARAH. You and your Roman trinkets! I hate serving them.
I'd like to spit in their cups each time I serve them.

LEAH. You wouldn't dare!

SARAH. Wouldn't I, though?
[*There are steps on the stairs as the innkeeper comes down*]

INNKEEPER. Here, here,
What's this, what's this, why are you standing idle?
They're calling for more wine!

SARAH. Let Leah serve them.
She likes their looks!

WIFE. Sarah!

[13]

SARAH [*sighs*]. Yes, mistress.

WIFE. Please, Sarah—we've talked like this so many times.

SARAH. Very well, mistress. But let her go first.
[*To Leah*]
Get up the stairs, you little soldier's comfort!
I hope he pinches you!

LEAH. Mistress, it's not my fault. Does Sarah have to—

WIFE. Oh go, go—both of you!
[*They mutter and go upstairs*]

INNKEEPER. Well, that's a pretty little tempest for you.
You ought to beat the girl. She's insolent
And shows it.

WIFE. We can't be too hard on her.
Her father's dead, her brother's in the hills,
And yet she used to be a merry child.
I can remember her when she was merry,
A long time since.

INNKEEPER. You always take their side
And yet, you'd think a self-respecting inn
Could have some decent and well-mannered maids!
But no such luck—sullens and sluts, the lot of them!
Give me a stool—I'm tired.
[*He sits, muttering*]
Say thirty dinners
And double for the prefect—and the wine—
Best, second best and common—h'm, not bad
But then—
[*Suddenly*]

Why do you sit there, staring at the fire,
So silent and so waiting and so still?
   [*Unearthly music, very faint at first, begins with the
   next speech and builds through the scene*]

   WIFE. I do not know. I'm waiting.

   INNKEEPER. Waiting for what?

   WIFE. I do not know. For something new and
      strange,
Something I've dreamt about in some deep sleep,
Truer than any waking,
Heard about, long ago, so long ago,
In sunshine and the summer grass of childhood,
When the sky seems so near.
I do not know its shape, its will, its purpose
And yet all day its will has been upon me,
More real than any voice I ever heard,
More real than yours or mine or our dead child's,
More real than all the voices there upstairs,
Brawling above their cups, more real than light.
And there is light in it and fire and peace,
Newness of heart and strangeness like a sword,
And all my body trembles under it,
And yet I do not know.

   INNKEEPER. You're tired, my dear.
Well, we shall sleep soon.

   WIFE. No, I am not tired.
I am expectant as a runner is
Before a race, a child before a feast day,
A woman at the gates of life and death,
Expectant for us all, for all of us
Who live and suffer on this little earth

With such small brotherhood.   Something begins.
Something is full of change and sparkling stars.
Something is loosed that changes all the world.
   [*Music up and down*]
And yet—I cannot read it yet.   I wait
And strive—and cannot find it.
   [*A knock at the door*]
Hark?   What's that?

   INNKEEPER.   They can't come in.   I don't care who
      they are.
We have no room.
   [*Knock is repeated*]

   WIFE.   Go to the door!
   [*He goes and opens the door*]

   INNKEEPER.   Well?
   [*Strain of music*]

   JOSEPH [*from outside*].   Is this the inn?   Sir, we are
      travelers
And it is late and cold.   May we enter?

   WIFE [*eagerly*].   Who is it?

   INNKEEPER [*to her*].   Just a pair of country people,
A woman and a man.   I'm sorry for them
But—

   JOSEPH.   My wife and I are weary.
May we come in?

   INNKEEPER.   I'm sorry, my good man.
We have no room tonight.   The prefect's orders.

   JOSEPH.   No room at all?

   INNKEEPER.   Now, now, it's not my fault.
You look like honest and well-meaning folk

And nobody likes turning trade away
But I'm not my own master.   Not tonight.
It may be, in the morning—
   [*He starts to close the door*]

   WIFE.   Wait!

   INNKEEPER [*in a fierce whisper*].   Must you mix in this?

   WIFE.   Wait!
   [*She goes to the door*]
Good sir, the enemy are in our house
And we—
   [*She sees the Virgin, who does not speak throughout
      this scene but is represented by music*]
   WIFE.   Oh.
   [*Music*]
   WIFE [*haltingly*].   I—did not see your wife.   I did not
      know.

   JOSEPH [*simply*].   Her name is Mary.   She is near her
      time.

   WIFE.   Yes.   Yes.
   [*To the innkeeper*]
Go—get a lantern.
Quickly!

   INNKEEPER.   What?

   WIFE.   Quickly!
   [*To Joseph and Mary*]
I—I once had a child.
We have no room.   That's true.
And it would not be right.   Not here.   Not now.
Not with those men whose voices you can hear,
Voices of death and iron.—King Herod's voices.

Better the friendly beasts. What am I saying?
There is—we have a stable at the inn,
Safe from the cold, at least—and, if you choose,
You shall be very welcome. It is poor
But the poor share the poor their crumbs of bread
Out of God's hand, so gladly,
And that may count for something. Will you share it?

    JOSEPH. Gladly and with great joy.

    WIFE. The lantern, husband!

    JOSEPH. Nay, I will take it. I can see the path.
Come!
    [*Music up. Joseph and Mary go. Innkeeper and wife watch them*]

    INNKEEPER [*to wife*]. Well, I suppose that you must have your way
And, any other night —— They're decent people
Or seem to be—

    WIFE. He has his arm about her, smoothing out
The roughness of the path for her.

    INNKEEPER. —Although
They are not even people of our town,
As I suppose you know—

    WIFE. So rough a path to tread with weary feet!

    INNKEEPER. Come in.
    [*He shivers*]
Brr, there's a frost upon the air tonight.
I'm cold or—yes, I must be cold. That's it.
That's it, now, to be sure. Come, shut the door.

    WIFE. Something begins, begins;
Starlit and sunlit, something walks abroad

In flesh and spirit and fire.
Something is loosed to change the shaken world.
   [*Music up and down. A bell strikes the hour*]

   NARRATOR. The night deepens. The stars march in
      the sky.
The prefect's men are gone. The inn is quiet
Save for the sleepy servants and their mistress,
Who clean the last soiled pots.
The innkeeper drowses before the fire.
But, in the street, outside—
   [*Music, changing into a shepherd's carol*]

   1ST SHEPHERD. As we poor shepherds watched by
      night

   CHORUS. With a hey, with a ho.

   1ST SHEPHERD. A star shone over us so bright
We left our flocks to seek its light

   CHORUS. In excelsis deo,
Gloria, gloria,
In excelsis deo.

   1ST SHEPHERD. We left our silly sheep to stray,

   CHORUS. With a hey, with a ho.

   1ST SHEPHERD. They'll think us no good shepherds,
      they.
And yet we came a blessed way.

   CHORUS. In excelsis deo,
Gloria, gloria,
In excelsis deo.

   1ST SHEPHERD. Now how may such a matter be?

CHORUS. With a hey, with a ho.

1ST SHEPHERD. That we of earth, poor shepherds we,
May look on Jesu's majesty?
And yet the star says—"It is He!"

2ND SHEPHERD. It is He!

3RD SHEPHERD. It is He!

CHORUS. Sing excelsis deo!
Gloria, gloria
In excelsis deo!

SARAH. Who sings so late? How can they sing so late?

LEAH. I'll go and see.
Wait—I'll rub the windowpane.
It's rimed with frost.
  [*She looks out*]
They're shepherds from the hills.

WIFE. Shepherds?

LEAH. Yes, mistress. They have crooks and staves.
Their tattered cloaks are ragged on their backs.
Their hands are blue and stinging with the cold
And yet they all seem drunken, not with wine
But with good news. Their faces shine with it.

WIFE. Cold—and so late. Poor creatures—call them
   in.
The prefect's men are gone.

LEAH. Aye but—the master—

WIFE. He's dozing. Do as I tell you.

LEAH [*calling out*]. Come in—come in—tarry a while
   and rest!

SHEPHERDS [*joyously*]. We cannot stay. We follow
    the bright star.
Gloria, gloria
In excelsis deo!

WIFE. Where did they go? Would they not stay with
    us?
Not one?

LEAH. Mistress, they did not even look on me.
They looked ahead. They have gone toward the stable,
The stable of our inn.

WIFE. The stable of our inn. And they are gone.

LEAH [*excitedly*]. Aye—gone but—Mistress! Mistress!
    Do you hear?

WIFE. Hear what?

LEAH. The tread of steeds on the hard ground,
Iron-hoofed, ringing clear—a company
That comes from out the East. I've never seen
Such things. I am afraid. These are great lords,
Great kings, with strange and memorable beasts,
And crowns upon their heads!

INNKEEPER [*waking*]. What's that? What's that?
Lords, nobles, kings, here in Bethlehem,
In our poor town? What fortune! O, what fortune!
Stand from the window there, you silly girl,
I'll speak to them!
    [*He calls out*]
My gracious noble masters,
Worthy and mighty kings! Our humble inn
Is honored by your high nobility!
Come in—come in—we've fire and beds and wine!
Come in—come in—tarry awhile and rest!

KINGS' VOICES [*joyfully*]. We cannot stay! We follow
   the bright star!
Gloria, gloria
In excelsis deo!

   INNKEEPER. I do not understand it. They are gone.
They did not even look at me or pause
Though there's no other inn.
They follow the poor shepherds to the stable.

   WIFE. They would not tarry with us—no, not one.

   INNKEEPER. And yet—

   WIFE. Peace, husband. You know well enough
Why none would tarry with us.
And so do I. I lay awhile in sleep
And a voice said to me, "Gloria, gloria,
Gloria in excelsis deo.
The child is born, the child, the child is born!"
And yet I did not rise and go to him,
Though I had waited and expected long,
For I was jealous that my child should die
And her child live.
And so—I have my judgment. And it is just.

   INNKEEPER. Dreams.

   WIFE. Were they dreams, the shepherds and the kings?
Is it a dream, this glory that we feel
Streaming upon us—and yet not for us?

   LEAH. Now, mistress, mistress, 'tis my fault not yours.
You told me seek the strangers in the stable
And see they had all care but I—forgot.

   SARAH. Kissing your soldier!

   LEAH. Sarah!

SARAH. I am sorry, Leah.
My tongue's too sharp. Mistress, the fault was mine.
You told me also and I well remembered
Yet did not go.

WIFE. Sarah.

SARAH. I did not go.
Brooding on mine own wrongs, I did not go.
It was my fault.

INNKEEPER. If there was any fault, wife, it was mine.
I did not wish to turn them from my door
And yet—I know I love the chink of money,
Love it too well, the good, sound, thumping coin,
Love it—oh, God, since I am speaking truth,
Better than wife or fire or chick or child,
Better than country, better than good fame,
Would sell my people for it in the street,
Oh, for a price—but sell them.
And there are many like me. And God pity us.

WIFE. God pity us indeed, for we are human,
And do not always see
The vision when it comes, the shining change,
Or, if we see it, do not follow it,
Because it is too hard, too strange, too new,
Too unbelievable, too difficult,
Warring too much with common, easy ways,
And now I know this, standing in this light,
Who have been half alive these many years,
Brooding on my own sorrow, my own pain,
Saying "I am a barren bough. Expect
Nor fruit nor blossom from a barren bough."
Life is not lost by dying! Life is lost
Minute by minute, day by dragging day,

In all the thousand, small, uncaring ways,
The smooth appeasing compromises of time,
Which are King Herod and King Herod's men,
Always and always. Life can be
Lost without vision but not lost by death,
Lost by not caring, willing, going on
Beyond the ragged edge of fortitude
To something more—something no man has seen.
You who love money, you who love yourself,
You who love bitterness, and I, who loved
And lost and thought I could not love again,
And all the people of this little town,
Rise up! The loves we had were not enough.
Something is loosed to change the shaken world,
And with it we must change!

    [*The voice of Dismas, the thief, breaking in—a rather
    quizzical, independent voice*]

    DISMAS. Now that's well said!

    INNKEEPER. Who speaks there? Who are you?

    DISMAS. Who? Oh, my name is Dismas. I'm a thief.
You know the starved, flea-bitten sort of boy
Who haunts dark alleyways in any town,
Sleeps on a fruit sack, runs from the police,
Begs what he can and—borrows what he must.
That's me!

    INNKEEPER. How did you get here?

    DISMAS. By the door, innkeeper,
The cellar door. The lock upon it's old.
I could pick locks like that when I was five.

    INNKEEPER. What have you taken?

    DISMAS. Nothing.

I tried the stable first—and then your cellar,
Slipped in, crept up, rolled underneath a bench,
While all your honest backs were turned—and then—

    WIFE. And then?

    DISMAS. Well—something happened. I don't know what.
I didn't see your shepherds or your kings,
But, in the stable, I did see the child,
Just through a crack in the boards—one moment's space.
That's all that I can tell you.
    [*Passionately*]
Is he for me as well? Is he for me?

    WIFE. For you as well.

    DISMAS. Is he for all of us?
There are so many of us, worthy mistress,
Beggars who show their sores and ask for alms,
Women who cough their lungs out in the cold,
Slaves—oh, I've been one!—thieves and runagates
Who knife each other for a bite of bread,
Having no other way to get the bread,
—The vast sea of the wretched and the poor,
Whose murmur comes so faintly to your ears
In this fine country.
Has he come to all of us
Or just to you?

    WIFE. To every man alive.

    DISMAS. I wish I could believe.

    SARAH [*scornfully*]. And, if you did,
No doubt you'd give up thieving!

    DISMAS. Gently, lady, gently.

Thieving's my trade—the only trade I know.
But, if it were true,
If he had really come to all of us—
I say, to all of us—
Then, honest man or thief,
I'd hang upon a cross for him!
  [*A shocked pause. The others mutter*]

  DISMAS. Would *you?*
  [*Another pause*]
I see that I've said something you don't like,
Something uncouth and bold and terrifying,
And yet, I'll tell you this:
It won't be till each one of us is willing,
Not you, not me, but every one of us,
To hang upon a cross for every man
Who suffers, starves and dies,
Fight his sore battles as they were our own,
And help him from the darkness and the mire,
That there will be no crosses and no tyrants,
No Herods and no slaves.
  [*Another pause*]
Well, it was pleasant, thinking things might be so.
And so I'll say farewell. I've taken nothing.
And he was a fair child to look on.

  WIFE. Wait!

  DISMAS. Why? What is it you see there, by the
    window?

  WIFE. The dawn, the common day,
The ordinary, poor and mortal day.
The shepherds and the kings have gone away.
The great angelic visitors are gone.
He is alone. He must not be alone.

INNKEEPER. I do not understand you, wife.

DISMAS. Nor I.

WIFE. Do you not see, because I see at last?
Dismas, the thief, is right.
He comes to all of us or comes to none.
Not to my heart in joyous recompense
For what I lost—not to your heart or yours,
But to the ignorant heart of all the world,
So slow to alter, so confused with pain.
Do you not see he must not be alone?

INNKEEPER. I think that I begin to see. And yet—

WIFE. We are the earth his word must sow like wheat
And, if it finds no earth, it cannot grow.
We are his earth, the mortal and the dying,
Led by no star—the sullen and the slut,
The thief, the selfish man, the barren woman,
Who have betrayed him once and will betray him,
Forget his words, be great a moment's space
Under the strokes of chance,
And then sink back into our small affairs.
And yet, unless *we* go, his message fails.

LEAH. Will he bring peace, will he bring brotherhood?

WIFE. He would bring peace, he would bring brother-
    hood
And yet he will be mocked at in the street.

SARAH. Will he slay King Herod
And rule us all?

WIFE. He will not slay King Herod. He will die.
There will be other Herods, other tyrants,
Great wars and ceaseless struggles to be free,
Not always won.

INNKEEPER. These are sad tidings of him.

WIFE. No, no—they are glad tidings of great joy,
Because he brings man's freedom in his hands,
Not as a coin that may be spent or lost
But as a living fire within the heart,
Never quite quenched—because he brings to all,
The thought, the wish, the dream of brotherhood,
Never and never to be wholly lost,
The water and the bread of the oppressed,
The stay and succor of the resolute,
The harness of the valiant and the brave,
The new word that has changed the shaken world.
And, though he die, his word shall grow like wheat
And every time a child is born,
In pain and love and freedom hardly won,
Born and gone forth to help and aid mankind,
There will be women with a right to say
"Gloria, gloria in excelsis deo!
A child is born!"

SARAH. Gloria!

LEAH. Gloria!

WIFE. Come, let us go. What can we bring to him?
What mortal gifts?

LEAH [*shyly*]. I have a ribbon. It's my prettiest.
It is not much but—he might play with it.

SARAH. I have a little bell my father gave me.
It used to make me merry. I have kept it.
I—he may have it.

DISMAS. My pocket's empty and my rags are bare.
But I can sing to him. That's what I'll do
And—if he needs a thief to die for him—

INNKEEPER. I would give all my gold.
I will give my heart.

WIFE. And I my faith through all the years and years,
Though I forget, though I am led astray,
Though, after this I never see his face,
I will give all my faith.
Come, let us go,
We, the poor earth but we, the faithful earth,
Not yet the joyful, not yet the triumphant,
But faithful, faithful, through the mortal years!
Come!
[*Music begins*]

DISMAS [*sings*]. Come, all ye faithful.

INNKEEPER. Joyful and triumphant.

WOMEN. Come ye, O come ye to Bethlehem!
[*Their voices rise in chorus in "Come, all ye faithful."
The chorus and the music swell.*]

The Tinker

By Dr. Fred Eastman. A new comedy in three acts. Four men, three women. One set—a living room. Plays two hours and a quarter.

The story centers upon a lonely man of wealth, who decides to rid himself of his possessions and devote the remainder of his life to service. His first opportunity for service presents itself unexpectedly in the materialistic household of his nephew, whom he has not seen for twenty years. Disguised as a tinker he enters the nephew's home and brings to it a new spirit. The drama is brightened with flashes of real humor, and the action moves swiftly to a strong climax.

"... a very religious drama, although there is little or no mention of religion in it. There is much clever dialog, the action moves briskly to a satisfying climax, and the whole play seems to be well adapted for either professional or amateur production."—The Christian Century.

"THE TINKER is compelling; it swept me off my feet! I thank you a thousand times for writing it. It fitted into my theme with one of my classes today so that I boldly quoted from it."—Dr. George Albert Coe.

"THE TINKER which I directed for the Columbia Federation of Baptist Young People's Unions was a great success. The audience numbered nine hundred and the comments and criticisms have been most gratifying. It is truly a great play and well worth the effort put forth in producing it."—L. G. P., Washington, D. C.

"The play went over beautifully. It was a joy to see it so, for I have the honor of having first played the rôle of TINKER under Dr. Eastman's direction at Chicago Theological Seminary. It is hard to turn over a loved rôle to another. But the director's part also yields its thrills."—L. W., Holyoke, Colorado.

"THE TINKER is a splendid drama."—Rev. R. H. C., Charles City, Iowa.

Royalty, $15.00. Price, 85 Cents.

Suggestions for Easter

HE IS NOT HERE! HE IS RISEN. By PAUL NAGY, JR. Containing "A Service for the Dedication of an Easter Garden," The Ritual of "The Kindling of the Holy Fire." Cast: according to size of production. Scene: Joseph's garden, Jerusalem. For either an outdoor sunrise service or the chancel. The purpose of the Service is to remind ourselves that even as Christ arose from the dead, so the grave holds no terror, death no victory. "The Kindling of the Flame" is a dramatization of an ancient legend and is based on the Scripture verse: "I am come to send fire on the earth." It represents Jesus as the Light of the World.

                                        Price, 50 Cents

MY FATHER'S BUSINESS. Play in two acts and optional epilogue. By CHRISTINE HUBBARD PICKETT. Six men, six women, one child (two extra women and voice of Jesus in epilogue). Interior. One hour. Suitable for Easter when given with epilogue. A play dealing with the home life of Jesus in his early twenties. The problem is whether the Elder Brother should take advantage of the opportunity to study at the temple in Jerusalem, or stay in Nazareth to help his recently widowed mother. The decision is determined by his necessity to devote himself to the Father's business. Although Jesus never appears on the stage, his personality dominates words and action. It is so genuine and natural that the play will act extraordinarily well.

Royalty, $5.00   Price, 50 Cents

A CLOUD OF WITNESSES. By ESTHER WILLARD BATES. Five men, seven women and a group of singers. The setting is a chancel of a church on Easter Sunday. Some of the characters are in the world and others have transcended mortal life. The happy spirits of three devoted church members have returned, unseen and unheard except by each other and the audience, to participate in the Resurrection Day Service, and to convey, mysteriously, yet beautifully, their supreme knowledge of immortality. Choir music, the minister's words and Bible verse combine in a triumphant assurance of everlasting life.

Royalty, $5.00   Price, 50 Cents

Baker's Plays: BOSTON 16, MASS.
                                    and
                                Denver 2, Colorado

A DRAMATIC
Presentation of Religion
CAN SWAY THE HEART AND
ENCOURAGE THE DEED

THE BIBLE COMES ALIVE. Twelve Biblical Sermons in Costume. By NORMAN E. NYGAARD. No elaborate preparations are necessary and the costuming is simple. These sermons are given through the medium of short plays, the minister portraying the principal character in each one, through whom the message is given. With the needful spiritual preparation, both on the part of the minister and of all others who participate in the services, these messages can be real blessings to a congregation.   Price, $1.00

EASY BIBLE STORY DRAMATIZATIONS FOR CHILDREN. By KARIN SUNDELOF-ASBRAND. This book has been written to bring clear and interesting pictures of Bible drama before the eyes of the young. Each one is vivid in color and dramatic enough to hold the interest of child and adult alike yet simple to produce and easy to learn.   Price, $1.00

EASY CHURCH PLAYS FOR CHILDREN. By various authors. A fine group of short plays for Sunday School and church clubs, written for children between the ages of four and twelve. Most of them call for no costumes or special staging but they are worth doing and the children will enjoy them.   Price, $1.00

EASY PROGRAMS FOR MOTHER'S DAY. Edited by THEODORE JOHNSON. 156 pages of fine plays, platform readings, a little pageant, a suggestion for banquets, a drill and miscellaneous material.   Price, $1.00

EASY SUNDAY SCHOOL ENTERTAINMENTS. By KARIN SUNDELOF-ASBRAND. A high quality omnibus collection of genuinely worthwhile program material for Easter—Christmas—Mother's Day—Father's Day—Children's Day and Rally Day, Plays and miscellaneous programs—if they are the right kind—are a natural means of both expression and instruction for the child.
Price, $1.00

LIVING HYMNS. By EDITH H. WILLIS and EDITH ELLSWORTH. Presenting in Choral Drama the centuries of struggle which lie behind our best-loved hymns and the men and women who wrote them. Two narrators and chorus or choirs. May be a complete one hour program or four twenty-minute presentations.
Price, **75 Cents**

Baker's Plays:
BOSTON   MASS.
and
Denver 2, Colorado

Three Plays Reflecting the Best in

Religious Drama

DESIGN FOR A STAINED GLASS WINDOW. *Play by* WILLIAM BERNEY *and* HOWARD RICHARDSON. 9 men—3 women, extras. Interior. Royalty, $25.00. Books, 85 Cents each.

Here is the story of the making of a potential Saint, in the life story of Margaret Clitherow, an English woman who actually lived in the time of Queen Elizabeth. Margaret was baptized as a child in the Catholic Church, but at the age of ten when Elizabeth turned against Pope Pius V, Margaret and the rest of her family, except her father, became Conformists and joined the Protestant cause. Circumstances and associations lead Margaret to re-embrace the Catholic religion. Because in a jury trial her husband and children would have to testify against her, she refuses to plead to the charges. The crown having declared all Catholics to be traitors, she is given a traitor's sentence—death by torture.

SPARK IN JUDEA. *By* R. F. DELDERFIELD. 10 men—3 women. Scene: The reception chamber used by Pontius Pilate during his temporary residence in Jerusalem. Period: Circa 33 A. D. Period costumes. Royalty, $25.00. Books, 85 Cents each.

Ever since the death and Resurrection of Christ 20 centuries ago, the background of His Passion has been one of the most fruitful for the playwright. So often, though, in plays of this type, it is difficult to avoid the melodramatic, the saccharine-sweet, the obvious. SPARK IN JUDEA happily works no such "silver tears" of overwrought emotionalism. It could almost be called a political drama, with the personage of Christ, the "harmless philosopher," being just one of the difficulties that came up daily upon the legal ledger of the governor of Judea and Samaria. Yet Pilate knows this Jewish carpenter, who calls himself a King, is no ordinary man. Thus, in actuality, it is the mind of Pontius Pilate, enigmatic, wavering, frightened—that becomes the focal dramatic issue of the play.

JOYFUL MYSTERY. Five Episodes in Choric Verse. *By* JOHN L. BONN, S.J. Stylized settings. 11 speaking parts, 10 chorus. Books, 75 Cents each.

The following review of Fr. Bonn's play tells better than we can the tremendous impact of the message of this great dramatic poem: "I think that it meant something individual to every one who saw it. To me it has always meant Man's soul plunged into darkness by the sin of Adam, groping blindly through the ages toward the light."

BAKER'S PLAYS   Boston 16, Massachusetts

Suggestions for Christmas

CELEBRATING CHRISTMAS. Collected and Edited by Edna M. Cahill. When one gets to thinking of the mistletoe and holly, of the tree with its trimmings, of Santa and the merriment of the holiday season one usually gets to thinking, too, of entertainment for the happy get-togethers of school, church, club at this festive time. As our title suggests our collection is especially for these occasions. It contains just about everything in the way of program material—plays, worship service, pantomime, exercises, monologues, recitations, stunts and games. There's material suited to children as well as adults; some of it is serious in theme, most of it merely to add gaiety to the holiday spirit. *Price,* $1.00.

* * *

ROSES FOR THE KING. Christmas Phantasy. By Hazel F. Bailey. 3 w., 2 m., and several children. No scenery. Here's a charming play appealing to adult and child alike. It seems that in this warring world its gentle but firm message will be pertinent for some time to come. In fact, the play is so simple that it must be beautifully done with understanding. Written for reading aloud pleasure as well as for acting. *Price,* 50 Cents.

* * *

TO US A SON. Drama. By J. Paul Faust. 3 m., several shepherds, 7 w. Int. 30 min. There is a decided freshness to this re-telling of the story of "no room in the inn." Joshua, the serious-minded son of Jacob and Mara, finds hope in the words of the prophet Isaiah when everyone is threatening and plotting to break the yoke of Rome. *Price,* 50 Cents.

Baker's Plays

Boston 16, Massachusetts   Denver 2, Colorado

www.ingramcontent.com/pod-product-compliance
Lightning Source LLC
Chambersburg PA
CBHW031819110426
42743CB00057B/990